How to Live on 24 Hours a Day
by
Arnold Bennett

아놀드 베넷 시간 관리론

How to Live on 24 Hours a Day

1판 1쇄 발행 2008년 6월 5일
1판 3쇄 발행 2009년 3월 20일

지은이 | 아놀드 베넷
해설 | 서재영
펴낸이 | 박찬영
기획편집 | 이인석, 김혜경, 한미정
마케팅 | 이진규, 장민영
디자인 | 이창욱

발행처 | 리베르
주소 | 서울시 용산구 용산동5가 24번지 용산파크타워 103동 505호
등록번호 | 제2003-43호
전화 | 02-790-0587, 0588
팩스 | 02-790-0589
홈페이지 | www.liberbooks.co.kr
커뮤니티 | blog.naver.com/liber_book(블로그)
　　　　　cafe.naver.com/talkinbook(카페)
e-mail | skyblue7410@hanmail.net

리베르(LIBER)는 디오니소스 신에 해당하며 책과 전원의 신을 의미합니다.
또한 liberty(자유), library(도서관)의 어원으로서 자유와 지성을 상징합니다.

How to Live on 24 Hours a Day
by

Arnold Bennett

아놀드 베넷 지음 | 서재영 해설

리베르

머리말

시간 관리의 바이블로 전세계적으로 널리 읽히는 아놀드 베넷의 『하루 24시간을 사는 법 How to Live on 24 Hours a Day』의 영문판이 한글 번역본과 함께 국내 처음으로 출간되었다. 무엇보다 이 책은 아주 평이한 문체로 쓰여 있다. 문장이 복잡하지 않아서 고등학생 수준의 영어 실력을 가진 독자라면 누구나 읽기에 무리가 없다. 따라서 이 소책자는 문법 해설 없이 영어 텍스트를 어느 정도 자유롭게 읽어 갈 수 있는 독자들에게는 더할 나위 없는 영어 학습 교재이자 자기계발서의 역할을 동시에 할 수 있을 것이다. 보다 정확한 이해를 위해 한글 번역본을 참고할 수도 있겠다.

아놀드 베넷의 문장은 문어체와 구어체가 적절히 섞

여 있다. 이 책의 내용은 원래 영국의 한 일간지에 연재된 것으로서 독자와 대화하는 스타일을 취하면서도 고풍스러운 문어체를 적절히 가미해 그 품격을 높이고 있다. 독자들은 이 원문을 읽으면서 한 예술가의 잔잔하면서도 힘 있는 필치를 느낄 수 있을 것이다. 정통 영국식 영어로 되어 있으므로 영어 원본의 운치를 느끼고자 하는 독자분들에게도 추천하고 싶다.

『How to Live on 24 Hours a Day』 한글판 (『시간관리론』)

역자 서재영

Contents

머리말 • 4
어휘 및 구문 (Word & Phrases) • 165

Preface • 7
Chapter 1   The Daily Miracle • 27
Chapter 2   The Desire to Exceed One's Programme • 39
Chapter 3   Precautions before Beginning • 51
Chapter 4   The Cause of the Trouble • 63
Chapter 5   Tennis and the Immortal Soul • 75
Chapter 6   Remember Human Nature • 87
Chapter 7   Controlling the Mind • 97
Chapter 8   The Reflective Mood • 109
Chapter 9   Interest in the Arts • 121
Chapter 10 Nothing in Life is Humdrum • 133
Chapter 11 Serious Reading • 143
Chapter 12 Dangers to Avoid • 155

Preface

This preface, though placed at the beginning, as a preface must be, should be read at the end of the book.

I have received a large amount of correspondence concerning this small work, and many reviews of it—some of them nearly as long as the book itself—have been printed. But scarcely any of the comment has been adverse. Some people have objected to a frivolity of tone; but as the tone is not, in my opinion, at all frivolous, this objection did not impress me; and had no weightier reproach been put forward I might almost have been persuaded that the volume was flawless! A more serious stricture has, however, been offered—not in the press, but by sundry obviously sincere correspondents—and I must deal with it. A reference to page 66 will show that I anticipated and feared this disapprobation. The sentence against which protests have been made is as follows:—"In the majority of instances he [the typical man] does not precisely feel a passion for his business; at best he does not dislike it. He begins his business functions with some reluctance, as late as he can, and he ends them with joy, as early as he can. And his engines, while he is engaged in his business, are seldom at their full 'h.p.'"

I am assured, in accents of unmistakable sincerity, that there are many business men—not merely those in high positions or with fine prospects, but modest subordinates with no hope of ever being much better off—who do enjoy their business functions, who do not shirk them, who do not arrive at the office as late as possible and depart as early as possible, who, in a word, put the whole of their force into their day's work and are genuinely fatigued at the end thereof.

I am ready to believe it. I do believe it. I know it. I always knew it. Both in London and in the provinces it has been my lot to spend long years in subordinate situations of business; and the fact did not escape me that a certain proportion of my peers showed what amounted to an honest passion for their duties, and that while engaged in those duties they were really *living* to the fullest extent of which they were capable. But I remain convinced that these fortunate and happy individuals (happier perhaps than they gue-

ssed) did not and do not constitute a majority, or anything like a majority. I remain convinced that the majority of decent average conscientious men of business (men with aspirations and ideals) do not as a rule go home of a night genuinely tired. I remain convinced that they put not as much but as little of themselves as they conscientiously can into the earning of a livelihood, and that their vocation bores rather than interests them.

Nevertheless, I admit that the minority is of sufficient importance to merit attention, and that I ought not to have ignored it so completely as I did do. The whole difficulty of the hard-working minority was put in a single colloquial sentence by one of my correspondents. He wrote: "I am just as keen as anyone on doing something to 'exceed my programme,' but allow me to tell you that when I get home at six thirty p.m. I am not anything like so fresh as you seem to imagine."

Now I must point out that the case of the minority, who throw themselves with passion and gusto into their daily business task, is infinitely less deplorable than the case of the majority, who go half-heartedly and feebly through their official day. The former are less in need of advice "how to live." At any rate during their official day of, say, eight hours they are really alive; their engines are giving the full indicated "h.p." The other eight working hours of their day may be badly organised, or even frittered away; but it is less disastrous to waste eight hours a day than sixteen hours a day; it is better to have lived a bit than never to have lived at all. The real tragedy is the tragedy of the man who is braced to effort neither in the office nor out of it, and to this man this book is primarily addressed. "But," says the other and more

fortunate man, "although my ordinary programme is bigger than his, I want to exceed my programme too! I am living a bit; I want to live more. But I really can't do another day's work on the top of my official day."

The fact is, I, the author, ought to have foreseen that I should appeal most strongly to those who already had an interest in existence. It is always the man who has tasted life who demands more of it. And it is always the man who never gets out of bed who is the most difficult to rouse.

Well, you of the minority, let us assume that the intensity of your daily money-getting will not allow you to carry out quite all the suggestions in the following pages. Some of the suggestions may yet stand. I admit that you may not be able to use the time spent on the journey home at night; but the suggestion for the journey to the office in the morning is as practicable for you as for anybody. And that weekly interval of forty hours, from Saturday to Monday, is yours just as much as the other man's, though a slight accumulation of fatigue may prevent you from employing the whole of your "h.p." upon it. There remains, then, the important portion of the three or more evenings a week. You tell me flatly that you are too tired to do anything outside your programme at night. In reply to which I tell you flatly that if your ordinary day's work is thus exhausting, then the balance of your life is wrong and must be adjusted. A man's powers ought not to be monopolised by his ordinary day's work. What, then, is to be done?

The obvious thing to do is to circumvent your ardour for your ordinary day's work by a ruse. Employ your engines in something beyond the programme before, and not after, you employ them on the programme itself. Briefly, get up earlier in the morning. You

say you cannot. You say it is impossible for you to go earlier to bed of a night—to do so would upset the entire household. I do not think it is quite impossible to go to bed earlier at night. I think that if you persist in rising earlier, and the consequence is insufficiency of sleep, you will soon find a way of going to bed earlier. But my impression is that the consequence of rising earlier will not be an insufficiency of sleep. My impression, growing stronger every year, is that sleep is partly a matter of habit—and of slackness. I am convinced that most people sleep as long as they do because they are at a loss for any other diversion. How much sleep do you think is daily obtained by the powerful healthy man who daily rattles up your street in charge of Carter Paterson's van? I have consulted a doctor on this point. He is a doctor who for twenty-five years has had a large general practice in a large flourishing suburb of London, inhabited by exactly such people as you and me. He is a curt man, and his answer was curt:

"Most people sleep themselves stupid."

He went on to give his opinion that nine men out of ten would have better health and more fun out of life if they spent less time in bed.

Other doctors have confirmed this judgment, which, of course, does not apply to growing youths.

Rise an hour, an hour and a half, or even two hours earlier; and—if you must—retire earlier when you can. In the matter of exceeding programmes, you will accomplish as much in one morning hour as in two evening hours. "But," you say, "I couldn't begin without some food, and servants." Surely, my dear sir, in an age when an excellent spirit-lamp (including a saucepan) can be bought for less than a shilling, you are not going to

allow your highest welfare to depend upon the precarious immediate co-operation of a fellow creature! Instruct the fellow creature, whoever she may be, at night. Tell her to put a tray in a suitable position over night. On that tray two biscuits, a cup and saucer, a box of matches and a spirit-lamp; on the lamp, the saucepan; on the saucepan, the lid—but turned the wrong way up; on the reversed lid, the small teapot, containing a minute quantity of tea leaves. You will then have to strike a match—that is all. In three minutes the water boils, and you pour it into the teapot (which is already warm). In three more minutes the tea is infused. You can begin your day while drinking it. These details may seem trivial to the foolish, but to the thoughtful they will not seem trivial. The proper, wise balancing of one's whole life may depend upon the feasibility of a cup of tea at an unusual hour.

A. B.

Chapter
1

The Daily Miracle

하루 24시간이라는 고귀한 시간

"Yes, he's one of those men that don't know how to manage. Good situation. Regular income. Quite enough for luxuries as well as needs. Not really extravagant. And yet the fellow's always in difficulties. Somehow he gets nothing out of his money. Excellent flat—half empty! Always looks as if he'd had the brokers in. New suit—old hat! Magnificent necktie—baggy trousers! Asks you to dinner: cut glass—bad mutton, or Turkish coffee—cracked cup! He can't understand it.

Explanation simply is that he fritters his income away. Wish I had the half of it! I'd show him—"

So we have most of us criticised, at one time or another, in our superior way.

We are nearly all chancellors of the exchequer: it is the pride of the moment. Newspapers are full of articles explaining how to live on such-and-such a sum, and these articles provoke a correspondence whose violence proves the interest they excite. Recently, in a daily organ, a battle raged round the question whether a woman can exist nicely in the country on £85 a year. I have seen an essay, "How to live on eight shillings a week." But I have never seen an essay, "How to live on twenty-four hours a day." Yet it has been said that time is money. That proverb understates the case. Time is a great deal more than money. If you have time you can obtain money—usually. But though you have the wealth of a cloak-room attendant at the Carlton Hotel, you cannot buy yourself a minute more time than I have, or the cat by the fire has.

Philosophers have explained space. They have not explained time. It is the inexplicable raw material of everything. With it, all is possible; without it, nothing. The supply of time is truly a daily miracle, an affair genuinely astonishing when one examines it. You wake up in the morning, and lo! your purse is magically filled with twenty-four hours of the unmanufactured tissue of the

universe of your life! It is yours. It is the most precious of possessions. A highly singular commodity, showered upon you in a manner as singular as the commodity itself!

For remark! No one can take it from you. It is unstealable. And no one receives either more or less than you receive.

Talk about an ideal democracy! In the realm of time there is no aristocracy of wealth, and no aristocracy of intellect. Genius is never rewarded by even an extra hour a day. And there is no punishment. Waste your infinitely precious commodity as much as you will, and the supply will never be withheld from you. No mysterious power will say:—"This man is a fool, if not a knave. He does not deserve time; he shall be cut off at the meter." It is more certain than consols, and payment of income is not affected by Sundays. Moreover, you cannot draw on the future. Impossible to get into debt! You can only waste the passing moment. You cannot waste tomorrow; it is kept for you. You cannot waste the next hour; it is kept for you.

I said the affair was a miracle. Is it not?

You have to live on this twenty-four hours of daily time. Out of it you have to spin health, pleasure, money, content, respect, and the evolution of your immortal soul. Its right use, its most effective use, is a matter of the highest urgency and of the most thrilling actuality. All depends on that. Your happiness—the elusive prize that you are all clutching for, my friends!—depends on that. Strange that the newspapers, so enterprising and up-to-date as they are, are not full of "How to live on a given income of time," instead of "How to live on a given income of money"! Money is far commoner than time. When one reflects, one perceives that money is just about the commonest thing there is. It encumbers the earth in gross heaps.

If one can't contrive to live on a certain income of money, one earns a little more—or steals it, or advertises for it. One doesn't necessarily muddle one's life because one can't quite manage on a thousand pounds a year; one braces the muscles and makes it guineas, and balances the budget. But if one cannot arrange that an income of twenty-four hours a day shall exactly cover all proper items of expenditure, one does muddle one's life definitely. The supply of time, though gloriously regular, is cruelly restricted.

Which of us lives on twenty-four hours a day? And when I say "lives," I do not mean exists, nor "muddles through." Which of us is free from that uneasy feeling that the "great spending departments" of his daily life are not managed as they ought to be? Which of us is quite sure that his fine suit is not surmounted by a shameful hat, or that in attending to the crockery he has forgotten the quality of the food? Which of us is not saying to himself—which of us has not been saying to himself all his life: "I shall alter that when I have a little more time"?

We never shall have any more time. We

have, and we have always had, all the time there is. It is the realisation of this profound and neglected truth (which, by the way, I have not discovered) that has led me to the minute practical examination of daily time-expenditure.

"

Don't say you don't have enough time. You have exactly the same number of hours per day that were given to Helen Keller, Pasteur, Michaelangelo, Mother Teresea, Leonardo da Vinci, Thomas Jefferson, and Albert Einstein.

"

_ H. Jackson Brown, Jr.

Chapter 2

The Desire to Exceed One's Programme

내 안에 잠자고 있는 열망

"But," someone may remark, with fine English disregard of everything except the point, "what is he driving at with his twenty-four hours a day? I have no difficulty in living on twenty-four hours a day. I do all that I want to do, and still find time to go in for newspaper competitions. Surely it is a simple affair, knowing that one has only twenty-four hours a day, to content one's self with twenty-four hours a day!"

To you, my dear sir, I present my excuses

and apologies. You are precisely the man that I have been wishing to meet for about forty years. Will you kindly send me your name and address, and state your charge for telling me how you do it? Instead of me talking to you, you ought to be talking to me. Please come forward. That you exist, I am convinced, and that I have not yet encountered you is my loss. Meanwhile, until you appear, I will continue to chat with my companions in distress—that innumerable band of souls who are haunted, more or less painfully, by the feeling that the years slip by, and slip by, and slip by, and that they have not yet been able to get their lives into proper working order.

If we analyse that feeling, we shall perceive it to be, primarily, one of uneasiness, of expectation, of looking forward, of aspiration. It is a source of constant discomfort, for it behaves like a skeleton at the feast of all our enjoyments. We go to the theatre and laugh; but between the acts it raises a skinny finger at us. We rush violently for the last train, and while we are cooling a long age on the platform waiting for the last train, it promenades its bones up and down by our side and inquires: "O man, what hast thou done with thy youth? What art thou doing with thine age?" You may urge that this feeling of continuous looking forward, of aspiration, is part of life itself, and inseparable from life itself. True!

But there are degrees. A man may desire to go to Mecca. His conscience tells him that he ought to go to Mecca. He fares forth, either by the aid of Cook's, or unassisted; he may probably never reach Mecca; he may drown before he gets to Port Said; he may perish ingloriously on the coast of the Red Sea; his desire may remain eternally frustrate. Unfulfilled aspiration may always trouble him. But he will not be tormented in the same way as the man who, desiring to reach Mecca, and harried by the desire to reach Mecca, never leaves Brixton.

It is something to have left Brixton. Most of us have not left Brixton. We have not even taken a cab to Ludgate Circus and inquired from Cook's the price of a conducted tour. And our excuse to ourselves is that there are only twenty-four hours in the day.

If we further analyse our vague, uneasy aspiration, we shall, I think, see that it springs from a fixed idea that we ought to do something in addition to those things which we are loyally and morally obliged to do. We are obliged, by various codes written and unwritten, to maintain ourselves and our families (if any) in health and comfort, to pay our debts, to save, to increase our prosperity by increasing our efficiency. A task sufficiently difficult! A task which very few of us achieve! A task often beyond our skill! Yet, if we succeed in it, as we sometimes do, we are not satisfied; the skeleton is still with us.

And even when we realise that the task is beyond our skill, that our powers cannot cope with it, we feel that we should be less discontented if we gave to our powers, already overtaxed, something still further to do.

And such is, indeed, the fact. The wish to accomplish something outside their formal programme is common to all men who in the course of evolution have risen past a certain level.

Until an effort is made to satisfy that wish, the sense of uneasy waiting for something to start which has not started will remain to disturb the peace of the soul. That wish has been called by many names. It is one form of the universal desire for knowledge. And it is so strong that men whose whole lives have been given to the systematic acquirement of knowledge have been driven by it to overstep the limits of their programme in search of still more knowledge. Even Herbert Spencer, in

my opinion the greatest mind that ever lived, was often forced by it into agreeable little backwaters of inquiry.

I imagine that in the majority of people who are conscious of the wish to live—that is to say, people who have intellectual curiosity—the aspiration to exceed formal programmes takes a literary shape. They would like to embark on a course of reading. Decidedly the British people are becoming more and more literary. But I would point out that literature by no means comprises the whole field of knowledge, and that the disturbing thirst to improve one's self—to increase one's knowledge—may well be slaked quite apart from literature. With the various ways of slaking I shall deal later. Here I merely point out to those who have no natural sympathy with literature that literature is not the only well.

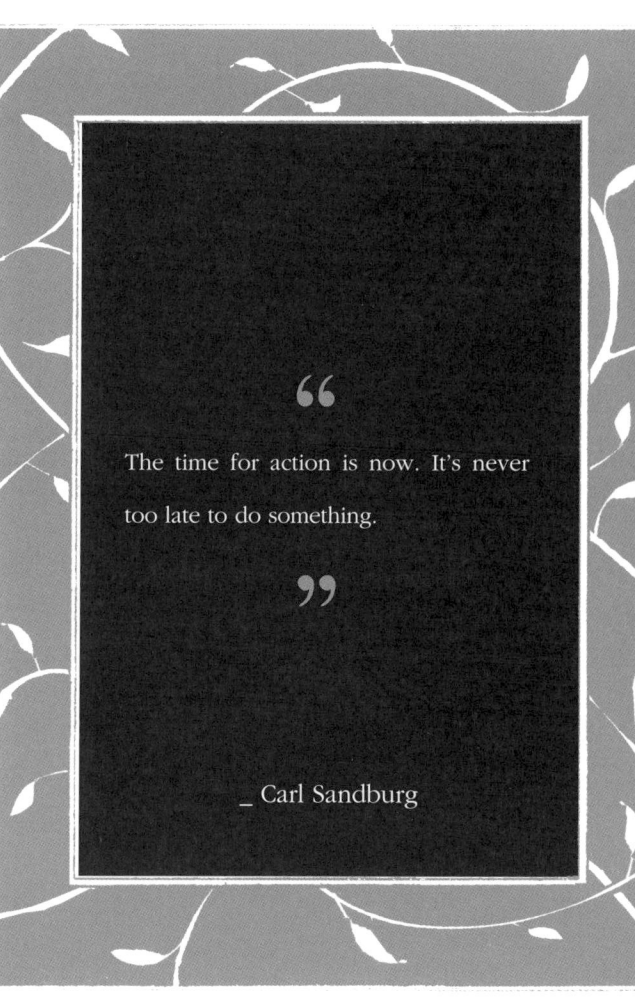

Chapter 3

Precautions before Beginning

지혜로운 시작을 위한 당부

Now that I have succeeded (if succeeded I have) in persuading you to admit to yourself that you are constantly haunted by a suppressed dissatisfaction with your own arrangement of your daily life; and that the primal cause of that inconvenient dissatisfaction is the feeling that you are every day leaving undone something which you would like to do, and which, indeed, you are always hoping to do when you have "more time"; and now that I have drawn your attention to the glaring, dazzling truth that you never will have "more time," since you already have all the time there is—you expect me to let you into some wonderful secret by which you may at any rate approach the ideal of a perfect arrangement of the day, and by which, therefore, that haunting, unpleasant, daily disappointment of things left undone will be got rid of!

I have found no such wonderful secret. Nor do I expect to find it, nor do I expect that anyone else will ever find it. It is undiscovered. When you first began to gather my drift, perhaps there was a resurrection of hope in your breast. Perhaps you said to yourself, "This man will show me an easy, unfatiguing way of doing what I have so long in vain wished to do." Alas, no! The fact is that there is no easy way, no royal road. The path to Mecca is extremely hard and stony, and the worst of it is that you never quite get there after all.

The most important preliminary to the task of arranging one's life so that one may live fully and comfortably within one's daily budget of twenty-four hours is the calm realisation of the extreme difficulty of the task, of the sacrifices and the endless effort which it demands. I cannot too strongly insist on this.

If you imagine that you will be able to achieve your ideal by ingeniously planning out a time-table with a pen on a piece of paper, you had better give up hope at once. If you are not prepared for discouragements and disillusions; if you will not be content with a small result for a big effort, then do not begin. Lie down again and resume the uneasy doze which you call your existence.

It is very sad, is it not, very depressing and sombre? And yet I think it is rather fine, too, this necessity for the tense bracing of the will before anything worth doing can be done. I rather like it myself. I feel it to be the chief thing that differentiates me from the cat by the fire.

"Well," you say, "assume that I am braced for the battle. Assume that I have carefully weighed and comprehended your ponderous remarks; how do I begin?" Dear sir, you simply begin. There is no magic method of beginning. If a man standing on the edge of a swimming-bath and wanting to jump into the cold water should ask you, "How do I begin to jump?" you would merely reply, "Just jump. Take hold of your nerves, and jump."

As I have previously said, the chief beauty about the constant supply of time is that you cannot waste it in advance. The next year, the next day, the next hour are lying ready for you, as perfect, as unspoilt, as if you had never wasted or misapplied a single moment in all your career. Which fact is very gratifying and reassuring. You can turn over a new leaf every hour if you choose. Therefore no object is served in waiting till next week, or even until tomorrow. You may fancy that the water will be warmer next week. It won't. It will be colder.

But before you begin, let me murmur a few words of warning in your private ear.

Let me principally warn you against your own ardour. Ardour in well-doing is a misleading and a treacherous thing. It cries out loudly for employment; you can't satisfy it at first; it wants more and more; it is eager to move mountains and divert the course of rivers. It isn't content till it perspires. And then, too often, when it feels the perspiration on its brow, it wearies all of a sudden and dies, without even putting itself to the trouble of saying, "I've had enough of this."

Beware of undertaking too much at the start. Be content with quite a little. Allow for accidents. Allow for human nature, especially your own.

A failure or so, in itself, would not matter, if it did not incur a loss of self-esteem and of self-confidence. But just as nothing succeeds like success, so nothing fails like failure. Most people who are ruined are ruined by attempting too much. Therefore, in setting out on the immense enterprise of living fully and comfortably within the narrow limits of twenty-four hours a day, let us avoid at any cost the risk of an early failure. I will not agree that, in this business at any rate, a glorious failure is better than a petty success. I am all for the petty success. A glorious failure leads to nothing; a petty success may lead to a success that is not petty.

So let us begin to examine the budget of the

day's time. You say your day is already full to overflowing. How? You actually spend in earning your livelihood—how much? Seven hours, on the average? And in actual sleep, seven? I will add two hours, and be generous. And I will defy you to account to me on the spur of the moment for the other eight hours.

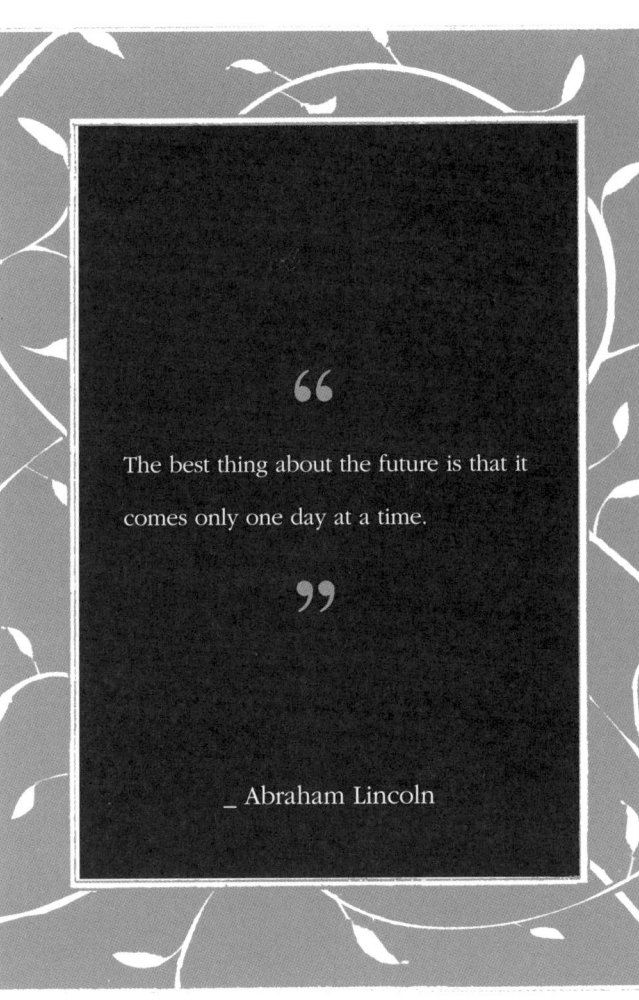

Chapter
4

The Cause of
the Trouble

잃어버린 시간을 되찾아라

In order to come to grips at once with the question of time-expenditure in all its actuality, I must choose an individual case for examination. I can only deal with one case, and that case cannot be the average case, because there is no such case as the average case, just as there is no such man as the average man. Every man and every man's case is special.

But if I take the case of a Londoner who works in an office, whose office hours are from ten to six, and who spends fifty minutes morning and night in travelling between his house door and his office door, I shall have got as near to the average as facts permit. There are men who have to work longer for a living, but there are others who do not have to work so long.

Fortunately the financial side of existence does not interest us here; for our present purpose the clerk at a pound a week is exactly as well off as the millionaire in Carlton House-terrace.

Now the great and profound mistake which my typical man makes in regard to his day is a mistake of general attitude, a mistake which vitiates and weakens two-thirds of his energies and interests. In the majority of instances he does not precisely feel a passion for his business; at best he does not dislike it. He begins his business functions with reluctance, as late as he can, and he ends them with joy, as early as he can. And his engines while he is engaged in his business are seldom at their full "h.p." (I know that I shall be accused by angry readers of traducing the city worker; but I am pretty thoroughly acquainted with the City, and I stick to what I say.)

Yet in spite of all this he persists in looking upon those hours from ten to six as "the day," to which the ten hours preceding them and the six hours following them are nothing but a prologue and an epilogue. Such an attitude, unconscious though it be, of course kills his interest in the odd sixteen hours, with the result that, even if he does not waste them, he

does not count them; he regards them simply as margin.

This general attitude is utterly illogical and unhealthy, since it formally gives the central prominence to a patch of time and a bunch of activities which the man's one idea is to "get through" and have "done with." If a man makes two-thirds of his existence subservient to one-third, for which admittedly he has no absolutely feverish zest, how can he hope to live fully and completely? He cannot.

If my typical man wishes to live fully and completely he must, in his mind, arrange a day within a day. And this inner day, a Chinese box in a larger Chinese box, must begin at 6 p.m. and end at 10 a.m. It is a day of sixteen hours; and during all these sixteen hours he has nothing whatever to do but cultivate his body and his soul and his fellow men. During those sixteen hours he is free; he is not a wage-earner; he is not preoccupied by monetary cares; he is just as good as a man with a private income. This must be his attitude. And his attitude is all important. His success in life (much more important than the amount of estate upon what his executors will have to pay estate duty) depends on it.

What? You say that full energy given to those sixteen hours will lessen the value of the business eight? Not so. On the contrary, it will assuredly increase the value of the business eight. One of the chief things which my typical man has to learn is that the mental faculties are capable of a continuous hard activity;

they do not tire like an arm or a leg. All they want is change—not rest, except in sleep.

I shall now examine the typical man's current method of employing the sixteen hours that are entirely his, beginning with his uprising. I will merely indicate things which he does and which I think he ought not to do, postponing my suggestions for "planting" the times which I shall have cleared—as a settler clears spaces in a forest.

In justice to him I must say that he wastes very little time before he leaves the house in the morning at 9.10. In too many houses he gets up at nine, breakfasts between 9.7 and 9.9½, and then bolts. But immediately he bangs the front door his mental faculties, which are tireless, become idle. He walks to the station

in a condition of mental coma. Arrived there, he usually has to wait for the train. On hundreds of suburban stations every morning you see men calmly strolling up and down platforms while railway companies unblushingly rob them of time, which is more than money. Hundreds of thousands of hours are thus lost every day simply because my typical man thinks so little of time that it has never occurred to him to take quite easy precautions against the risk of its loss.

He has a solid coin of time to spend every day—call it a sovereign. He must get change for it, and in getting change he is content to lose heavily.

Supposing that in selling him a ticket the company said, "We will change you a sovereign, but we shall charge you three halfpence for doing so," what would my typical man exclaim? Yet that is the equivalent of what the company does when it robs him of five minutes twice a day.

You say I am dealing with minutiae. I am. And later on I will justify myself.

Now will you kindly buy your paper and step into the train?

"

There is one kind of robber whom the law does not strike at, and who steals what is most precious to men: time.

"

_ Napoleon I

Chapter 5

Tennis and the Immortal Soul

몰입하는 아침, 설레는 저녁

You get into the morning train with your newspaper, and you calmly and majestically give yourself up to your newspaper. You do not hurry. You know you have at least half an hour of security in front of you. As your glance lingers idly at the advertisements of shipping and of songs on the outer pages, your air is the air of a leisured man, wealthy in time, of a man from some planet where there are a hundred and twenty-four hours a day instead of twenty-four. I am an impassioned reader of newspapers. I read five English and two French dailies, and the news-agents alone know how many weeklies, regularly. I am obliged to mention this personal fact lest I should be accused of a prejudice against newspapers when I say that I object to the reading of newspapers in the morning train. Newspapers are produced with rapidity, to be read with rapidity. There is no place in my daily programme for newspapers. I read them as I may in odd moments. But I do read them. The idea of devoting to them thirty or forty consecutive minutes of wonderful solitude (for nowhere can one more perfectly immerse one's self in one's self than in a compartment full of silent, withdrawn, smoking males) is to me repugnant. I cannot possibly allow you to scatter priceless pearls of time with such Oriental lavishness. You are not the Shah of time. Let me respectfully remind you that you have no more time than I have. No newspaper reading in trains! I have already "put by" about three-quarters of an hour for use.

Now you reach your office. And I abandon you there till six o'clock. I am aware that you have nominally an hour (often in reality an hour and a half) in the midst of the day, less than half of which time is given to eating. But I will leave you all that to spend as you choose. You may read your newspapers then.

I meet you again as you emerge from your office. You are pale and tired. At any rate, your wife says you are pale, and you give her to understand that you are tired. During the journey home you have been gradually working up the tired feeling. The tired feeling hangs heavy over the mighty suburbs of London like a virtuous and melancholy cloud, particularly in winter. You don't eat immediately on your arrival home. But in about an hour or so you feel as if you could sit up and take a little nourishment. And you do. Then you smoke, seriously; you see friends; you potter; you play cards; you flirt with a book; you note that old age is creeping on; you take a stroll; you caress the piano…… By Jove! a quarter past eleven. Time to think about going to bed! You then devote quite forty minutes to thinking about going to bed; and it is conceivable that you are acquainted with a genuinely good whisky. At last you go to bed, exhausted by the day's work. Six hours, probably more, have gone since you left the office—gone like a dream, gone like magic, unaccountably gone!

That is a fair sample case. But you say: "It's all very well for you to talk. A man *is* tired. A man must see his friends. He can't always be on the stretch." Just so. But when you arrange to go to the theatre (especially with a pretty woman) what happens? You rush to the suburbs; you spare no toil to make yourself glorious in fine raiment; you rush back to town in another train; you keep yourself on the stretch for four hours, if not five; you take her home; you take yourself home. You don't spend three-quarters of an hour in "thinking about" going to bed. You go. Friends and fatigue have equally been forgotten, and the evening has seemed so exquisitely long (or perhaps too short)! And do you remember that time when you were persuaded to sing in the chorus of the amateur operatic society, and slaved two hours every other night for three months? Can you deny that when you have something definite to look forward to at eventide, something that is to employ all your energy—the thought of that something gives a glow and a more intense vitality to the whole day?

What I suggest is that at six o'clock you look facts in the face and admit that you are not tired (because you are not, you know), and that you arrange your evening so that it is not cut in the middle by a meal. By so doing you

will have a clear expanse of at least three hours. I do not suggest that you should employ three hours every night of your life in using up your mental energy. But I do suggest that you might, for a commencement, employ an hour and a half every other evening in some important and consecutive cultivation of the mind. You will still be left with three evenings for friends, bridge, tennis, domestic scenes, odd reading, pipes, gardening, pottering, and prize competitions. You will still have the terrific wealth of forty-four hours between 2 p.m. Saturday and 10 a.m. Monday. If you persevere you will soon want to pass four evenings, and perhaps five, in some sustained endeavour to be genuinely alive. And you will fall out of that habit of muttering to yourself at 11.15 p.m., "Time to be thinking about going to bed." The man who begins to go to bed forty minutes before he opens his bedroom door is bored; that is to say, he is not living.

But remember, at the start, those ninety nocturnal minutes thrice a week must be the most important minutes in the ten thousand and eighty. They must be sacred, quite as sacred as a dramatic rehearsal or a tennis match. Instead of saying, "Sorry I can't see you, old chap, but I have to run off to the tennis club," you must say, "……but I have to work." This, I admit, is intensely difficult to say. Tennis is so much more urgent than the immortal soul.

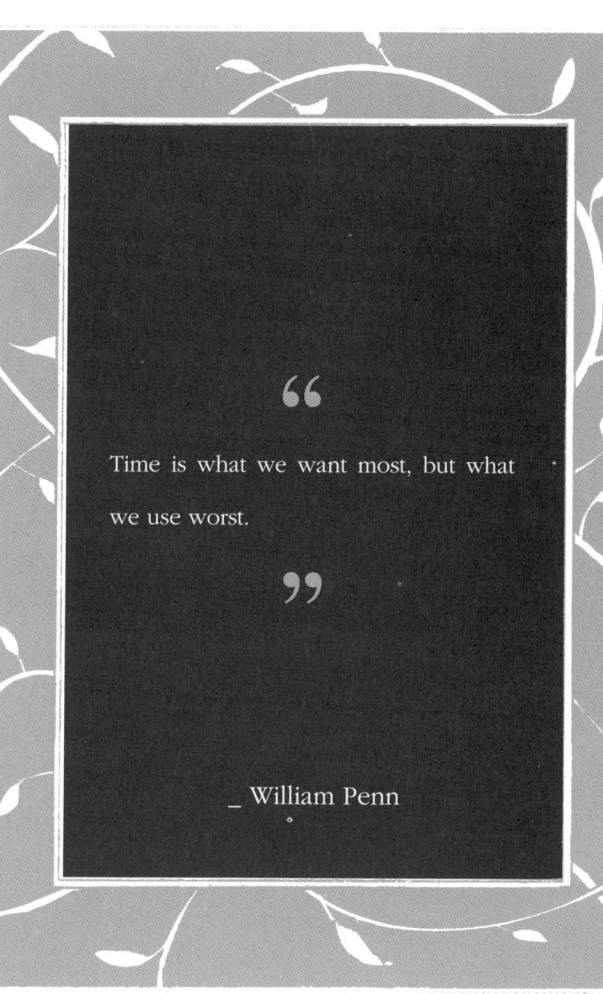

Chapter
6

Remember
Human Nature

일주일 단위로 계획하라

I have incidentally mentioned the vast expanse of forty-four hours between leaving business at 2 p.m. on Saturday and returning to business at 10 a.m. on Monday. And here I must touch on the point whether the week should consist of six days or of seven. For many years—in fact, until I was approaching forty—my own week consisted of seven days. I was constantly being informed by older and wiser people that more work, more genuine living, could be got out of six days than out of seven.

And it is certainly true that now, with one day in seven in which I follow no programme and make no effort save what the caprice of the moment dictates, I appreciate intensely the moral value of a weekly rest. Nevertheless, had I my life to arrange over again, I would do again as I have done. Only those who have lived at the full stretch seven days a week for a long time can appreciate the full beauty of a regular-recurring idleness. Moreover, I am ageing. And it is a question of age. In cases of abounding youth and exceptional energy and desire for effort I should say unhesitatingly: Keep going, day in, day out.

But in the average case I should say: Confine your formal programme (super-programme, I mean) to six days a week. If you find yourself wishing to extend it, extend it, but only in proportion to your wish; and count the time extra as a windfall, not as regular income, so that you can return to a six-day programme without the sensation of being poorer, of being a backslider.

Let us now see where we stand. So far we have marked for saving out of the waste of days, half an hour at least on six mornings a week, and one hour and a half on three evenings a week. Total, seven hours and a half a week.

I propose to be content with that seven hours and a half for the present. "What?" you cry. "You pretend to show us how to live, and you only deal with seven hours and a half out of a hundred and sixty-eight! Are you going to perform a miracle with your seven hours and a half?" Well, not to mince the matter, I am—if you will kindly let me! That is to say, I am going to ask you to attempt an experience which, while perfectly natural and explicable, has all the air of a miracle. My contention is that the full use of those seven-and-a-half hours will quicken the whole life of the week, add zest to it, and increase the interest which you feel in even the most banal occupations. You practise physical exercises for a mere ten minutes morning and evening, and yet you are not astonished when your physical health and strength are beneficially affected every hour of the day, and your whole physical outlook changed. Why should you be astonished that an average of over an hour a day given to the mind should permanently and completely enliven the whole activity of the mind?

More time might assuredly be given to the cultivation of one's self. And in proportion as the time was longer the results would be greater. But I prefer to begin with what looks like a trifling effort.

It is not really a trifling effort, as those will discover who have yet to essay it. To "clear" even seven hours and a half from the jungle is passably difficult. For some sacrifice has to be made. One may have spent one's time badly, but one did spend it; one did do something with it, however ill-advised that something may have been. To do something else means a change of habits.

And habits are the very dickens to change! Further, any change, even a change for the better, is always accompanied by drawbacks and discomforts. If you imagine that you will be able to devote seven hours and a half a week to serious, continuous effort, and still live your old life, you are mistaken. I repeat that some sacrifice, and an immense deal of volition, will be necessary. And it is because I know the difficulty, it is because I know the almost disastrous effect of failure in such an enterprise, that I earnestly advise a very humble beginning. You must safeguard your self-respect. Self-respect is at the root of all purposefulness, and a failure in an enterprise deliberately planned deals a desperate wound at one's self-respect. Hence I iterate and reiterate: Start quietly, unostentatiously.

When you have conscientiously given seven hours and a half a week to the cultivation of your vitality for three months—then you may begin to sing louder and tell yourself what wondrous things you are capable of doing.

Before coming to the method of using the indicated hours, I have one final suggestion to make. That is, as regards the evenings, to allow much more than an hour and a half in which to do the work of an hour and a half. Remember the chance of accidents. Remember human nature. And give yourself, say, from 9 to 11.30 for your task of ninety minutes.

I recommend to you to take care of the minutes; for hours will take care of themselves.

_ Lord Chesterfield

Chapter 7

Controlling the Mind

두뇌 훈련을 위한 조언

People say: "One can't help one's thoughts." But one can. The control of the thinking machine is perfectly possible. And since nothing whatever happens to us outside our own brain; since nothing hurts us or gives us pleasure except within the brain, the supreme importance of being able to control what goes on in that mysterious brain is patent. This idea is one of the oldest platitudes, but it is a platitude whose profound truth and urgency most people live and die without realising.

People complain of the lack of power to concentrate, not witting that they may acquire the power, if they choose.

And without the power to concentrate—that is to say, without the power to dictate to the brain its task and to ensure obedience—true life is impossible. Mind control is the first element of a full existence.

Hence, it seems to me, the first business of the day should be to put the mind through its paces. You look after your body, inside and out; you run grave danger in hacking hairs off your skin; you employ a whole army of individuals, from the milkman to the pig-killer, to enable you to bribe your stomach into decent behaviour. Why not devote a little attention to the far more delicate machinery of the mind, especially as you will require no extraneous aid? It is for this portion of the art and craft of living that I have reserved the time from the moment of quitting your door to the moment of arriving at your office.

"What? I am to cultivate my mind in the street, on the platform, in the train, and in the crowded street again?" Precisely. Nothing simpler! No tools required! Not even a book. Nevertheless, the affair is not easy.

When you leave your house, concentrate your mind on a subject (no matter what, to begin with). You will not have gone ten yards before your mind has skipped away under your very eyes and is larking round the corner with another subject.

Bring it back by the scruff of the neck. Ere

you have reached the station you will have brought it back about forty times. Do not despair. Continue. Keep it up. You will succeed. You cannot by any chance fail if you persevere. It is idle to pretend that your mind is incapable of concentration. Do you not remember that morning when you received a disquieting letter which demanded a very carefully-worded answer? How you kept your mind steadily on the subject of the answer, without a second's intermission, until you reached your office; whereupon you instantly sat down and wrote the answer? That was a case in which *you* were roused by circumstances to such a degree of vitality that you were able to dominate your mind like a tyrant. You would have no trifling. You insisted that its work should be done, and its work was done.

By the regular practice of concentration (as to which there is no secret—save the secret of perseverance) you can tyrannise over your mind (which is not the highest part of *you*) every hour of the day, and in no matter what place. The exercise is a very convenient one. If you got into your morning train with a pair of dumb-bells for your muscles or an encyclopaedia in ten volumes for your learning, you would probably excite remark. But as you walk in the street, or sit in the corner of the compartment behind a pipe, or "straphang" on the Subterranean, who is to know that you are engaged in the most important of daily acts? What asinine boor can laugh at

you?

I do not care what you concentrate on, so long as you concentrate. It is the mere disciplining of the thinking machine that counts. But still, you may as well kill two birds with one stone, and concentrate on something useful. I suggest—it is only a suggestion—a little chapter of Marcus Aurelius or Epictetus.

Do not, I beg, shy at their names. For myself, I know nothing more "actual," more bursting with plain common-sense, applicable to the daily life of plain persons like you and me (who hate airs, pose, and nonsense) than Marcus Aurelius or Epictetus. Read a chapter—and so short they are, the chapters!—in the evening and concentrate on it the next morning. You will see.

Yes, my friend, it is useless for you to try to disguise the fact. I can hear your brain like a telephone at my ear. You are saying to yourself: "This fellow was doing pretty well up to his seventh chapter. He had begun to interest me faintly. But what he says about thinking in trains, and concentration, and so on, is not for me. It may be well enough for some folks, but it isn't in my line."

It is for you, I passionately repeat; it is for you. Indeed, you are the very man I am aiming at.

Throw away the suggestion, and you throw away the most precious suggestion that was ever offered to you. It is not my suggestion. It is the suggestion of the most sensible, practical, hard-headed men that have walked the earth. I only give it you at second-hand. Try it. Get your mind in hand. And see how the process cures half the evils of life—especially worry, that miserable, avoidable, shameful disease—worry!

> Time is a sort of river of passing events, and strong is its current; no sooner is a thing brought to sight than it is swept by and another takes its place, and this too will be swept away.

_ Marcus Aurelius

Chapter
8

The Reflective Mood

하루 중 가장 소중한 시간

The exercise of concentrating the mind (to which at least half an hour a day should be given) is a mere preliminary, like scales on the piano. Having acquired power over that most unruly member of one's complex organism, one has naturally to put it to the yoke. Useless to possess an obedient mind unless one profits to the furthest possible degree by its obedience. A prolonged primary course of study is indicated.

Now as to what this course of study should

be there cannot be any question; there never has been any question. All the sensible people of all ages are agreed upon it. And it is not literature, nor is it any other art, nor is it history, nor is it any science. It is the study of one's self. Man, know thyself. These words are so hackneyed that verily I blush to write them. Yet they must be written, for they need to be written. (I take back my blush, being ashamed of it.) Man, know thyself. I say it out loud. The phrase is one of those phrases with which everyone is familiar, of which everyone acknowledges the value, and which only the most sagacious put into practice. I don't know why. I am entirely convinced that what is more than anything else lacking in the life of the average well-intentioned man of today is the reflective mood.

We do not reflect. I mean that we do not reflect upon genuinely important things: upon the problem of our happiness, upon the main direction in which we are going, upon what life is giving to us, upon the share which reason has (or has not) in determining our actions, and upon the relation between our principles and our conduct.

And yet you are in search of happiness, are you not? Have you discovered it?

The chances are that you have not. The chances are that you have already come to believe that happiness is unattainable. But men have attained it. And they have attained it by realising that happiness does not spring from the procuring of physical or mental pleasure, but from the development of reason and the adjustment of conduct to principles.

I suppose that you will not have the audacity to deny this. And if you admit it, and still devote no part of your day to the deliberate consideration of your reason, principles, and conduct, you admit also that while striving for a certain thing you are regularly leaving undone the one act which is necessary to the attainment of that thing.

Now, shall I blush, or will you?

Do not fear that I mean to thrust certain principles upon your attention. I care not (in this place) what your principles are. Your principles may induce you to believe in the righteousness of burglary. I don't mind. All I urge is that a life in which conduct does not

fairly well accord with principles is a silly life; and that conduct can only be made to accord with principles by means of daily examination, reflection, and resolution. What leads to the permanent sorrowfulness of burglars is that their principles are contrary to burglary. If they genuinely believed in the moral excellence of burglary, penal servitude would simply mean so many happy years for them; all martyrs are happy, because their conduct and their principles agree.

As for reason (which makes conduct, and is not unconnected with the making of principles), it plays a far smaller part in our lives than we fancy. We are supposed to be reasonable; but we are much more instinctive than reasonable. And the less we reflect, the less reasonable we shall be. The next time you get cross with the waiter because your steak is over-cooked, ask reason to step into the cabinet-room of your mind, and consult her. She will probably tell you that the waiter did not cook the steak, and had no control over the cooking of the steak; and that even if he alone was to blame, you accomplished nothing good by getting cross; you merely lost your dignity, looked a fool in the eyes of sensible men, and soured the waiter, while producing no effect whatever on the steak.

The result of this consultation with reason (for which she makes no charge) will be that when once more your steak is over-cooked you will treat the waiter as a fellow-creature, remain quite calm in a kindly spirit, and politely insist on having a fresh steak. The gain will be obvious and solid.

In the formation or modification of principles, and the practice of conduct, much help can be derived from printed books (issued at sixpence each and upwards). I mentioned in my last chapter Marcus Aurelius and Epictetus. Certain even more widely known works will occur at once to the memory. I may also mention Pascal, La Bruyere, and Emerson. For myself, you do not catch me travelling without my Marcus Aurelius. Yes, books are valuable. But not reading of books will take the place of a daily, candid, honest examination of what one has recently done, and what one is about to do—of a steady looking at one's self in the face (disconcerting though the sight may be).

When shall this important business be accomplished? The solitude of the evening journey home appears to me to be suitable for it. A reflective mood naturally follows the exertion of having earned the day's living. Of course if, instead of attending to an elementary and profoundly important duty, you prefer to read the paper (which you might just as well read while waiting for your dinner) I have nothing to say. But attend to it at some time of the day you must. I now come to the evening hours.

> If you want to make good use of your time, you've got to know what's most important and then give it all you've got.

_ Lee Iacocca

Chapter 9

Interest in the Arts

예술과 소통하라

Many people pursue a regular and uninterrupted course of idleness in the evenings because they think that there is no alternative to idleness but the study of literature; and they do not happen to have a taste for literature. This is a great mistake.

Of course it is impossible, or at any rate very difficult, properly to study anything whatever without the aid of printed books. But if you desired to understand the deeper depths of bridge or of boat-sailing you would not be deterred by your lack of interest in literature from reading the best books on bridge or boat-sailing. We must, therefore, distinguish between literature, and books treating of subjects not literary. I shall come to literature in due course.

Let me now remark to those who have never read Meredith, and who are capable of being unmoved by a discussion as to whether Mr. Stephen Phillips is or is not a true poet, that they are perfectly within their rights. It is not a crime not to love literature. It is not a sign of imbecility. The mandarins of literature will order out to instant execution the unfortunate individual who does not comprehend, say, the influence of Wordsworth on Tennyson. But that is only their impudence. Where would they be, I wonder, if requested to explain the influences that went to make Tschaikowsky's "Pathetic Symphony"?

There are enormous fields of knowledge quite outside literature which will yield magnificent results to cultivators. For example (since I have just mentioned the most popular piece of high-class music in England today), I am reminded that the Promenade Concerts begin in August. You go to them. You smoke your cigar or cigarette (and I regret to say that you strike your matches during the soft bars of the "Lohengrin" overture), and you enjoy the music. But you say you cannot play the piano or the fiddle, or even the banjo; that you know nothing of music.

What does that matter? That you have a genuine taste for music is proved by the fact that, in order to fill his hall with you and your peers, the conductor is obliged to provide programmes from which bad music is almost entirely excluded (a change from the old Covent Garden days!).

Now surely your inability to perform "The Maiden's Prayer" on a piano need not prevent you from making yourself familiar with the construction of the orchestra to which you listen a couple of nights a week during a couple of months! As things are, you probably think of the orchestra as a heterogeneous mass of instruments producing a confused agreeable mass of sound. You do not listen for details because you have never trained your ears to listen to details.

If you were asked to name the instruments which play the great theme at the beginning of the C minor symphony you could not name them for your life's sake. Yet you admire the C minor symphony. It has thrilled you. It will thrill you again. You have even talked about it, in an expansive mood, to that lady—you know whom I mean. And all you can positively state about the C minor symphony is that Beethoven composed it and that it is a "jolly fine thing."

Now, if you have read, say, Mr. Krehbiel's "How to Listen to Music" (which can be got at any bookseller's for less than the price of a stall at the Alhambra, and which contains photographs of all the orchestral instruments

and plans of the arrangement of orchestras) you would next go to a promenade concert with an astonishing intensification of interest in it. Instead of a confused mass, the orchestra would appear to you as what it is—a marvellously balanced organism whose various groups of members each have a different and an indispensable function. You would spy out the instruments, and listen for their respective sounds. You would know the gulf that separates a French horn from an English horn, and you would perceive why a player of the hautboy gets higher wages than a fiddler, though the fiddle is the more difficult instrument. You would *live* at a promenade concert, whereas previously you had merely existed there in a state of beatific coma, like a baby gazing at a bright object.

The foundations of a genuine, systematic knowledge of music might be laid. You might specialise your inquiries either on a particular form of music (such as the symphony), or on the works of a particular composer. At the end of a year of forty-eight weeks of three brief evenings each, combined with a study of programmes and attendances at concerts chosen out of your increasing knowledge, you would really know something about music, even though you were as far off as ever from jangling "The Maiden's Prayer" on the piano.

"But I hate music!" you say. My dear sir, I respect you.

What applies to music applies to the other arts. I might mention Mr. Clermont Witt's

"How to Look at Pictures," or Mr. Russell Sturgis's "How to Judge Architecture," as beginnings (merely beginnings) of systematic vitalising knowledge in other arts, the materials for whose study abound in London.

"I hate all the arts!" you say. My dear sir, I respect you more and more.

I will deal with your case next, before coming to literature.

But what minutes! Count them by sensation, and not by calendars, and each moment is a day.

_ Benjamin Disraeli

Chapter 10

Nothing in Life is Humdrum

세상은 재미로 가득하다

Art is a great thing. But it is not the greatest. The most important of all perceptions is the continual perception of cause and effect—in other words, the perception of the continuous development of the universe—in still other words, the perception of the course of evolution. When one has thoroughly got imbued into one's head the leading truth that nothing happens without a cause, one grows not only large-minded, but large-hearted.

It is hard to have one's watch stolen, but one

reflects that the thief of the watch became a thief from causes of heredity and environment which are as interesting as they are scientifically comprehensible; and one buys another watch, if not with joy, at any rate with a philosophy that makes bitterness impossible. One loses, in the study of cause and effect, that absurd air which so many people have of being always shocked and pained by the curiousness of life. Such people live amid human nature as if human nature were a foreign country full of awful foreign customs. But, having reached maturity, one ought surely to be ashamed of being a stranger in a strange land!

The study of cause and effect, while it lessens the painfulness of life, adds to life's picturesqueness. The man to whom evolution is but a name looks at the sea as a grandiose, monotonous spectacle, which he can witness in August for three shillings third-class return. The man who is imbued with the idea of development, of continuous cause and effect, perceives in the sea an element which in the day-before-yesterday of geology was vapour, which yesterday was boiling, and which tomorrow will inevitably be ice.

He perceives that a liquid is merely something on its way to be solid, and he is penetrated by a sense of the tremendous, changeful picturesqueness of life. Nothing will afford a more durable satisfaction than the constantly cultivated appreciation of this. It is the end of all science.

Cause and effect are to be found everywhere. Rents went up in Shepherd's Bush. It was painful and shocking that rents should go up in Shepherd's Bush. But to a certain point we are all scientific students of cause and effect, and there was not a clerk lunching at a Lyons Restaurant who did not scientifically put two and two together and see in the (once) Two-penny Tube the cause of an excessive demand for wigwams in Shepherd's Bush, and in the excessive demand for wigwams the cause of the increase in the price of wigwams.

"Simple!" you say, disdainfully. Everything—the whole complex movement of the universe—is as simple as that—when you can sufficiently put two and two together. And, my dear sir, perhaps you happen to be an estate agent's clerk, and you hate the arts, and you want to foster your immortal soul, and you can't be interested in your business because it's so humdrum.

Nothing is humdrum.

The tremendous, changeful picturesqueness of life is marvellously shown in an estate agent's office. What! There was a block of traffic in Oxford Street; to avoid the block people actually began to travel under the cellars and drains, and the result was a rise of rents in Shepherd's Bush! And you say that isn't picturesque! Suppose you were to study, in this spirit, the property question in London for an hour and a half every other evening. Would it not give zest to your business, and transform your whole life?

You would arrive at more difficult problems. And you would be able to tell us why, as the natural result of cause and effect, the longest straight street in London is about a yard and a half in length, while the longest absolutely straight street in Paris extends for miles. I think you will admit that in an estate agent's clerk I have not chosen an example that specially favours my theories.

You are a bank clerk, and you have not read that breathless romance (disguised as a scientific study), Walter Bagehot's "Lombard Street"? Ah, my dear sir, if you had begun with that, and followed it up for ninety minutes every other evening, how enthralling your business would be to you, and how much more clearly you would understand human nature.

You are "penned in town," but you love excursions to the country and the observation of wild life—certainly a heart-enlarging diversion. Why don't you walk out of your house door, in your slippers, to the nearest gas lamp of a night with a butterfly net, and observe the wild life of common and rare moths that is beating about it, and co-ordinate the knowledge thus obtained and build a superstructure on it, and at last get to *know* something about something?

You need not be devoted to the arts, nor to literature, in order to live fully.

The whole field of daily habit and scene is waiting to satisfy that curiosity which means life, and the satisfaction of which means an understanding heart.

I promised to deal with your case, O man who hates art and literature, and I have dealt with it. I now come to the case of the person, happily very common, who *does* "like reading."

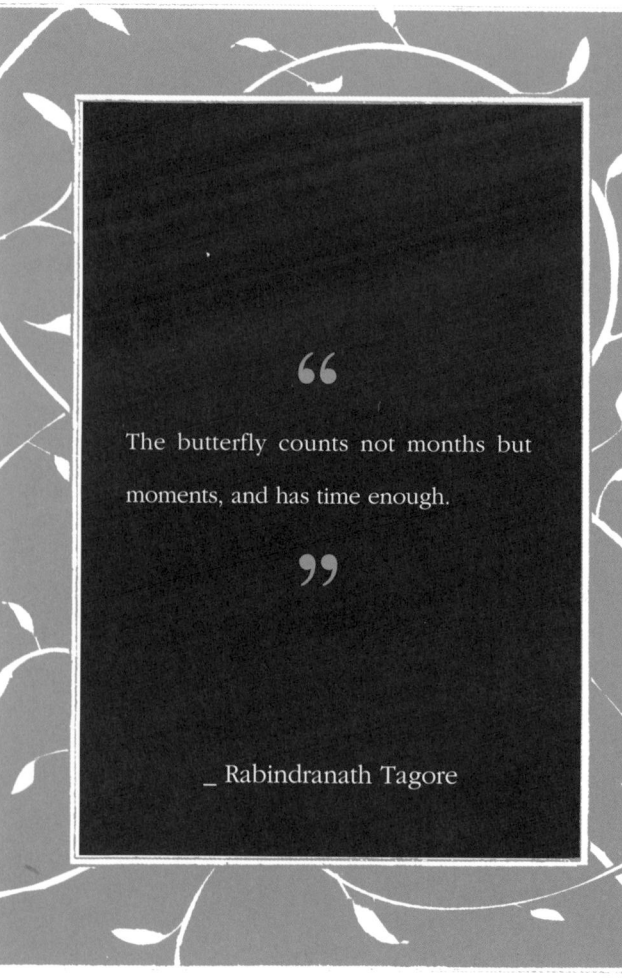

> The butterfly counts not months but moments, and has time enough.

_ Rabindranath Tagore

Chapter 11

Serious Reading

독서는 나의 힘

Novels are excluded from "serious reading," so that the man who, bent on self-improvement, has been deciding to devote ninety minutes three times a week to a complete study of the works of Charles Dickens will be well advised to alter his plans. The reason is not that novels are not serious—some of the great literature of the world is in the form of prose fiction—the reason is that bad novels ought not to be read, and that good novels never demand any appreciable mental application on the part of the reader. It is only the bad parts of Meredith's novels that are difficult. A good novel rushes you forward like a skiff down a stream, and you arrive at the end, perhaps breathless, but unexhausted. The best novels involve the least strain. Now in the cultivation of the mind one of the most important factors is precisely the feeling of strain, of difficulty, of a task which one part of you is anxious to achieve and another part of you is anxious to shirk; and that feeling cannot be got in facing a novel. You do not set your teeth in order to read "Anna Karenina." Therefore, though you should read novels, you should not read them in those ninety minutes.

Imaginative poetry produces a far greater

mental strain than novels. It produces probably the severest strain of any form of literature. It is the highest form of literature. It yields the highest form of pleasure, and teaches the highest form of wisdom. In a word, there is nothing to compare with it. I say this with sad consciousness of the fact that the majority of people do not read poetry.

I am persuaded that many excellent persons, if they were confronted with the alternatives of reading "Paradise Lost" and going round Trafalgar Square at noonday on their knees in sackcloth, would choose the ordeal of public ridicule. Still, I will never cease advising my friends and enemies to read poetry before anything.

If poetry is what is called "a sealed book" to

you, begin by reading Hazlitt's famous essay on the nature of "poetry in general." It is the best thing of its kind in English, and no one who has read it can possibly be under the misapprehension that poetry is a mediaeval torture, or a mad elephant, or a gun that will go off by itself and kill at forty paces. Indeed, it is difficult to imagine the mental state of the man who, after reading Hazlitt's essay, is not urgently desirous of reading some poetry before his next meal. If the essay so inspires you I would suggest that you make a commencement with purely narrative poetry.

There is an infinitely finer English novel, written by a woman, than anything by George Eliot or the Brontës, or even Jane Austen, which perhaps you have not read. Its title is

"Aurora Leigh," and its author E. B. Browning. It happens to be written in verse, and to contain a considerable amount of genuinely fine poetry. Decide to read that book through, even if you die for it. Forget that it is fine poetry. Read it simply for the story and the social ideas. And when you have done, ask yourself honestly whether you still dislike poetry. I have known more than one person to whom "Aurora Leigh" has been the means of proving that in assuming they hated poetry they were entirely mistaken.

Of course, if, after Hazlitt, and such an experiment made in the light of Hazlitt, you are finally assured that there is something in you which is antagonistic to poetry, you must be content with history or philosophy. I shall regret it, yet not inconsolably. "The Decline and Fall" is not to be named in the same day with "Paradise Lost," but it is a vastly pretty thing; and Herbert Spencer's "First Principles" simply laughs at the claims of poetry and refuses to be accepted as aught but the most majestic product of any human mind. I do not suggest that either of these works is suitable for a tyro in mental strains. But I see no reason why any man of average intelligence should not, after a year of continuous reading, be fit to assault the supreme masterpieces of history or philosophy. The great convenience of masterpieces is that they are so astonishingly lucid.

I suggest no particular work as a start. The attempt would be futile in the space at my command. But I have two general suggestions of a certain importance. The first is to define the direction and scope of your efforts. Choose a limited period, or a limited subject, or a single author. Say to yourself: "I will know something about the French Revolution, or the rise of railways, or the works of John Keats." And during a given period, to be settled beforehand, confine yourself to your choice. There is much pleasure to be derived from being a specialist.

The second suggestion is to think as well as to read. I know people who read and read, and for all the good it does them they might just as well cut bread-and-butter. They take to reading as better men take to drink. They fly through the shires of literature on a motor-car,

their sole object being motion. They will tell you how many books they have read in a year.

Unless you give at least forty-five minutes to careful, fatiguing reflection (it is an awful bore at first) upon what you are reading, your ninety minutes of a night are chiefly wasted. This means that your pace will be slow.

Never mind.

Forget the goal; think only of the surrounding country; and after a period, perhaps when you least expect it, you will suddenly find yourself in a lovely town on a hill.

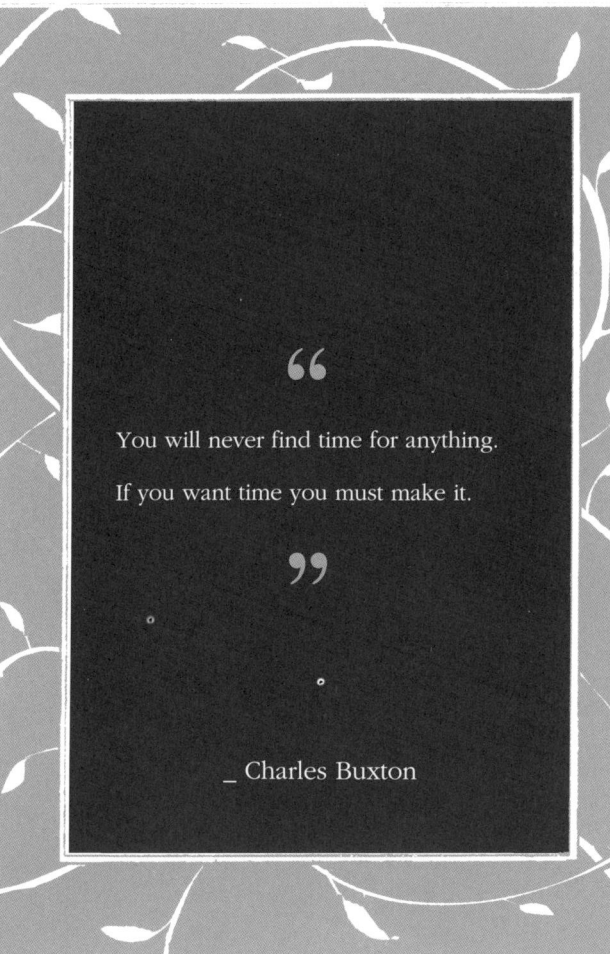

Chapter
12

Dangers to Avoid

앞길에 도사린 함정을 피하라

I cannot terminate these hints, often, I fear, too didactic and abrupt, upon the full use of one's time to the great end of living (as distinguished from vegetating) without briefly referring to certain dangers which lie in wait for the sincere aspirant towards life. The first is the terrible danger of becoming that most odious and least supportable of persons—a prig. Now a prig is a pert fellow who gives himself airs of superior wisdom. A prig is a pompous fool who has gone out for a ceremonial walk, and without knowing it has lost an important part of his attire, namely, his sense of humour. A prig is a tedious individual who, having made a discovery, is so impressed by his discovery that he is capable of being gravely displeased because the entire world is not also impressed by it. Unconsciously to become a prig is an easy and a fatal thing.

Hence, when one sets forth on the enterprise of using all one's time, it is just as well to remember that one's own time, and not other people's time, is the material with which one has to deal; that the earth rolled on pretty comfortably before one began to balance a budget of the hours, and that it will continue to roll on pretty comfortably whether or not one succeeds in one's new role of chancellor of the exchequer of time. It is as well not to chatter too much about what one is doing, and not to betray a too-pained sadness at the spectacle of a whole world deliberately wasting so many hours out of every day, and therefore never really living. It will be found, ultimately, that in taking care of one's self one has quite all one can do.

Another danger is the danger of being tied to a programme like a slave to a chariot. One's programme must not be allowed to run away with one. It must be respected, but it must not be worshipped as a fetish. A programme of daily employ is not a religion.

This seems obvious. Yet I know men whose lives are a burden to themselves and a distressing burden to their relatives and friends simply because they have failed to appreciate the obvious. "Oh, no," I have heard the martyred wife exclaim, "Arthur always takes the dog out for exercise at eight o'clock and he always begins to read at a quarter to nine. So it's quite out of the question that we should······" etc., etc. And the note of absolute finality in that plaintive voice reveals the unsuspected and ridiculous tragedy of a career.

On the other hand, a programme is a programme. And unless it is treated with deference it ceases to be anything but a poor joke. To treat one's programme with exactly the right amount of deference, to live with not too much and not too little elasticity, is scarcely the simple affair it may appear to the inexperienced.

And still another danger is the danger of developing a policy of rush, of being gradually more and more obsessed by what one has to do next. In this way one may come to exist as in a prison, and one's life may cease to be one's own. One may take the dog out for a walk at eight o'clock, and meditate the whole time on the fact that one must begin to read at a quarter to nine, and that one must not be late.

And the occasional deliberate breaking of one's programme will not help to mend matters. The evil springs not from persisting without elasticity in what one has attempted, but from originally attempting too much, from filling one's programme till it runs over. The only cure is to reconstitute the programme, and to attempt less.

But the appetite for knowledge grows by what it feeds on, and there are men who come to like a constant breathless hurry of endeavour. Of them it may be said that a constant breathless hurry is better than an eternal doze.

In any case, if the programme exhibits a tendency to be oppressive, and yet one wishes not to modify it, an excellent palliative is to pass with exaggerated deliberation from one portion of it to another; for example, to spend five minutes in perfect mental quiescence between chaining up the St. Bernard and opening the book; in other words, to waste five minutes with the entire consciousness of wasting them.

The last, and chiefest danger which I would indicate, is one to which I have already referred—the risk of a failure at the commencement of the enterprise.

I must insist on it.

A failure at the commencement may easily kill outright the newborn impulse towards a complete vitality, and therefore every precaution should be observed to avoid it. The impulse must not be over-taxed. Let the pace of the first lap be even absurdly slow, but let it be as regular as possible.

And, having once decided to achieve a certain task, achieve it at all costs of tedium and distaste. The gain in self-confidence of having accomplished a tiresome labour is immense.

Finally, in choosing the first occupations of those evening hours, be guided by nothing whatever but your taste and natural inclination.

It is a fine thing to be a walking encyclopaedia of philosophy, but if you happen to have no liking for philosophy, and to have a liking for the natural history of street-cries, much better leave philosophy alone, and take to street-cries.

> In theory one is aware that the earth revolves, but in practice one does not perceive it, the ground upon which one treads seems not to move, and one can live undisturbed. So it is with Time in one's life.

_ Marcel Proust

How to Live on 24 Hours a Day
Arnold Bennett

Words & Phrases

서문

correspondence 편지, 서신 왕래

concerning …에 관하여

adverse 반대하는, 거스르는

object 반대하다, 이의를 제기하다

frivolity 경박함

frivolous 경박한

weighty 설득력 있는

reproach 비난, 질책

flawless 흠 없는, 완벽한

stricture 비난, 혹평

sundry 갖가지의

obviously 명백하게, 분명하게

correspondent 편지 보낸 사람, 발신인

reluctance 마지못해 함, 꺼림

h.p.(=horse power) 마력

sincerity 진심, 정직, 성실

shirk (일, 의무, 책임 등을) 회피하다, 게으름 피우다

peer 동료

vocation 직업, 생업

keen on …을 열망하는

gusto 기호, 취미

deplorable 통탄할, 한탄스러운, 비참한

feebly 힘없이

fritter away (시간, 돈, 정력 등을) 조금씩 낭비하다

disastrous 비참한, 피해가 막심한

brace 긴장시키다

accumulation 축적

flatly 단호하게, 딱 잘라

monopolise 독점하다

circumvent 우회하다, 포위하다

ruse 책략, 계략

persist 지속하다, 계속하다

consequence 결과

insufficiency 부족

slackness 느슨함, 태만

diversion 기분 전환, 오락

rattle up (차가) 덜걱거리며 달리다

flourishing 번화한

inhabit …에 살다, 거주하다

curt 무뚝뚝한, 퉁명스러운

spirit-lamp 알코올 램프

saucepan 긴 손잡이가 달리고 뚜껑이 있는 깊은 냄비

precarious 불확실한, 믿을 수 없는

saucer 받침 접시

infuse (차를) 우리다

trivial 사소한, 하찮은

feasibility 실행할 수 있음, (실행) 가능성

CHAPTER 1

extravagant 낭비하는, 사치스러운

broker 전당포 업자

magnificent 아주 멋진, 최고급의

baggy 헐렁헐렁한, 불룩한

cut glass 컷글라스(표면을 조각한 크리스탈 유리그릇)

mutton 양고기

Turkish coffee 달게 먹는 짙은 가루 커피

cracked 금이 간

chancellor (영)장관, 대법관

exchequer (영)재무부, 재정경제부

provoke 유발하다

daily organ 일간 신문

rage 고조에 달하다

understate (가치나 수량을) 실제보다 줄여서 말하다

cloak-room (호텔·극장 등의) 외투류(휴대품) 보관소

attendant 안내원, 시중 드는 사람

inexplicable 설명할 수 없는

singular 기이한, 기괴한

commodity 상품, 일용품, 필수품

realm 영역, 범위

aristocracy 귀족, 상류[특권] 계급

intellect 지성

withhold 보류하다

knave 악한, 악당

consol 상환 기한이 없고 정기적으로 이자만 치르면 되는 공채

spin 이끌어 내다, 만들어 내다

content 만족감

immortal 불멸의, 영원한

urgency 긴급, 절박

thrilling 떨리는, 가슴 뛰게 하는

actuality 현실, 실제

elusive (교묘히) 피하는, 잡히지 않는

clutch 잡으려 들다

enterprising 진취적인

up-to-date 최신의, 첨단의

encumber (방해물로 장소를) 막다

gross 커다란, 엄청난

heap (쌓아 올린) 더미, 무더기

contrive 그럭저럭 …을 해내다

not necessarily 반드시 …한 것은 아니다

muddle 뒤죽박죽(엉망)으로 만들다

guinea 영국의 옛 금화

expenditure 지출, 소비, 비용

gloriously 기가 막히게, 기분이 썩 좋게

restrict 제한하다, 한정하다

muddle through (계획 없이) 그럭저럭 살아가다

surmount … 위에 얹다

crockery 도자기류

alter 달라지다, 변하다

profound 깊은, 심오한

neglect 무시하다, 등한시하다

minute 자세한, 세밀한

CHAPTER 2

exceed 넘어서다, 능가하다

with disregard of …을 무시하는 태도로

go in for …에 열중하다, 골몰하다

content 만족시키다

come forward 나서다, 앞으로 나오다

encounter 만나다, 마주치다

meanwhile 그 동안(사이)에

in distress 고민하는, 곤란해 하는

innumerable 셀 수 없이 많

은, 무수한

band (사람의) 무리

haunt 늘 따라다니다, 괴롭히다

slip by (시간이) 지나다

feast 축제

enjoyment 향락, 기쁨

act (연극의) 막

skinny 바싹 여윈

violently 맹렬하게, 세차게

promenade 보란 듯이 데리고 다니다

inseparable 분리할 수 없는, 뗄 수 없는

degree 정도, 단계

conscience 양심

fare forth 여행을 떠나다

Cook's 영국 여행사 Cook and Sons의 약어

unassisted 도움을 받지 않고

drown 물에 빠져 죽다

perish (갑자기) 죽다, 비명횡사하다

ingloriously 수치스럽게, 이름 없이

frustrate 좌절하다

unfulfilled 이루어지지 않은, 실현되지 않은

torment 괴롭히다, 고문하다

harry 괴롭히다, 귀찮게 요구하다

conduct 안내하다, 이끌다

vague 모호한, 막연한

loyally 충성스럽게

be obliged to …할 의무가 있다

prosperity 부유, 번창

efficiency 효율성

discontented 불만스러운, 불만을 품은

overtax 혹사하다, 무리하게 일을 시키다

systematic 체계적인

acquirement 습득, 획득

overstep (한도를) 넘다

agreeable 적당한

backwater 지적 부진(知的 不振), 침체

inquiry 탐구, 연구

embark on …에 착수하다

decidedly 확실히, 명백히

slake (갈증·욕망 등을) 만족시키다

CHAPTER 3

suppressed 억압된, 짓눌린

dissatisfaction 불만족

arrangement 정리, 정돈, 배열

primal 제1의, 주요한

glaring 번쩍번쩍 빛나는

dazzling 눈부신, 찬란한

drift 취지

resurrection 부활

breast 가슴

preliminary 사전 준비, 예비 행위

ingeniously 정교하게, 영리하게

disillusion 환멸

doze 졸기, 선잠

sombre 침울한, 우울한

differentiate 구별짓다, 차별화시키다

ponderous 지루하고 답답한

unspoilt 해를 입지 않은

misapply 잘못 사용하다, 오용

하다

gratifying 만족을 주는, 기분 좋은

reassuring 위안을 주는, 안심시키는

fancy 상상하다, 마음에 그리다

murmur 속삭이다, 중얼거리다

ardour 열정, 정열, 열심

well-doing 선행, 덕행

misleading 잘못 인도하는, 오도하는

treacherous 배반하는, 믿을 수 없는

divert 딴 데로 돌리다, 흐름을 바꾸다

perspire 땀을 흘리다

perspiration 발한(發汗) 작용, 땀

beware of …을 조심하다

undertake 착수하다, 시작하다

incur 초래하다

petty 작은, 보잘것없는

overflowing 차고 넘치는

livelihood 생계, 살림

account 설명하다, 밝히다

CHAPTER 4

vitiate 손상시키다, 해치다

traduce 비방하다, 중상하다

be acquainted with …에 정통하다, 잘 알다

stick to …을 고수하다

precede …보다 앞서다

odd 남은

utterly 완전히, 아주

prominence 두드러짐, 현저함

subservient 부차적인

feverish 열띤, 열광적인

zest 열정, 열성, 강한 흥미

wage-earner 임금 생활자, 근로자

be preoccupied by …에 몰두한, 정신이 팔린

monetary 금전상의, 재정상의

estate 소유지, 사유지

uprising 기상, 자리에서 일어남

settler 이주자, 개척자

bolt 뛰어나가다

tireless 지칠 줄 모르는

coma 혼수 상태

stroll 한가로이 거닐다

unblushingly 염치 없이, 얼굴 붉히지도 않고

sovereign 1파운드 금화 (현재는 사용하지 않음)

minutiae 사소한 일, 하찮은 세부 사항

CHAPTER 5

majestically 당당하게

security 안전, 안심

glance 흘긋 봄, 일견

linger 남아 있다, 꾸물거리다

idly 게으르게, 멍하니

leisured 한가한

impassioned 열렬한, 열정적인

daily 일간 신문

news-agent 신문 판매업자

prejudice 편견

with rapidity 신속히, 빠르게

odd 이따금의

consecutive 연속적인, 계속되는

repugnant 비위에 맞지 않는, 아주 싫은, 불유쾌한

scatter 흩뿌리다

priceless (값으로 따질 수 없을 만큼) 귀중한

lavishness 낭비, 헤픔, 풍부함

Shah 이란 국왕의 존칭

mighty 아주 큰

virtuous 고결한 체 하는

melancholy 음산한, 우울한

nourishment 음식

potter 빈둥거리다

creep 슬며시 다가오다

take a stroll 거닐다, 산책하다

caress 애무하다, 어루만지다

By Jove! 이런! 아이고! (감탄사)

conceivable 생각할 수 있는

genuinely 진정으로

on the stretch 긴장하여

spare 아끼다

toil 수고, 노고, 고생

raiment 의복, 복장

fatigue 피로, 피곤

eventide 저녁 무렵, 황혼

glow 흥분, 열정, 행복감

vitality 활력, 생명력

expanse 여유

commencement 시작, 개시

persevere 끈기 있게 노력하다

sustained 지속된, 한결 같은, 일관된

mutter 중얼거리다, 투덜거리다

nocturnal 밤의, 야간의

sacred 신성한, 성스러운

old chap 이 사람아!

CHAPTER 6

caprice 충동, 변덕

dictate 지시하다

age 나이를 먹다, 늙다

abounding 풍부한, 많은

day in, day out 날이면 날마다

confine 한정하다, 제한하다

windfall 뜻밖의 횡재, 굴러 들어온 복

backslider 퇴보자, 타락자

not to mince the matter 꾸밈없이 솔직히 말해서

explicable 설명할 수 있는

contention 주장, 논점

banal 평범한, 진부한

beneficially 유익하게

enliven 활기 있게 하다, 생기를 주다

passably 적당하게, 통과할 수 있게

trifling 하찮은, 시시한, 적은

jungle 정글, (대도시 등의) 번잡하고 소란한 곳

dickens 악마

drawback 약점, 결점

volition 의지, 결단

safeguard 보호하다

purposefulness 과단성, 결단

iterate 되풀이하다, 반복하다

unostentatiously 거만떨지 않고, 수수하게

wondrous 놀랄 만한

CHAPTER 7

supreme 최고의, 최상의

patent 명백한

platitude 평범한 의견, 상투어

ensure 확실하게 하다, 보증하다

hence 그러므로, 따라서

grave 중대한, 심각한

hack 짧게 깎다, 베며 나아가다

extraneous 외부의, 외래의

lark 희롱하다

scruff 목덜미

ere …하기 전에

disquieting 불안하게 하는, 걱정하게 하는

intermission 휴식 시간, 막간, 중단

rouse 환기하다, 깨우다

dominate 지배하다

tyrant 폭군, 전제 군주

compartment 구획, 칸막이

strap-hang (버스·지하철 따위로) 통근하다

on the Subteranean 지하철을 타고

asinine 어리석은, 고집 센

boor 예의를 모르는 (무례한) 남자

disguise (사실을) 숨기다, 감추다

faintly 어렴풋이, 희미하게

folk 사람들

sensible 분별 있는, 지각 있는

hard-headed 건전한 분별력을 지닌

at second-hand 간접적으로

CHAPTER 8

reflective 반성하는, 성찰하는

scale 음계

unruly 제멋대로 하는, 다루기 힘든

organism 유기체

yoke 멍에

hackneyed 낡은, 진부한

verily 진실로, 참으로

blush 얼굴을 붉히다, 부끄러워하다

acknowledge 인정하다

sagacious 현명한, 영리한, 슬기로운

attain 달성하다, 이루다, 성취하다

procure 획득하다

adjustment 조정, 조절, 수정

audacity 뻔뻔스러움, 무모함

deliberate 신중한, 사려 깊은

strive for …을 얻으려 애쓰다

attainment 달성, 도달

thrust 억지로 강요하다

induce …에게 어떤 행위를 하게 하다

righteousness 옳음, 정당성

burglary 도둑질, 강도

resolution 결단, 결심

penal 형벌의

servitude 징역

martyr 순교자

instinctive 본능적인, 반사적인

get cross 기분이 언짢아지다

dignity 존엄, 품위

sour 불쾌하게 만들다

consultation 상담, 상의, 자문

modification 변경, 조절

derive …에서 끌어내다

candid 솔직한, 숨김 없는

disconcerting 당황케 하는

exertion 노력, 격심한 활동

CHAPTER 9

uninterrupted 중단되지 않는, 연속된

idleness 게으름, 할 일 없음

alternative 대안

bridge 브리지(카드 놀이의 일종)

deter 그만두게 하다, 단념시키다

in due course 적당한 때에, 머지 않아

unmoved 태연한, 변동이 없는

imbecility 저능, 우둔함

impudence 뻔뻔스러움, 몰염치

pathetic 슬픈, 비창한

overture 서곡, 전주곡

fiddle 바이올린

banjo 밴조(현악기의 일종)

conductor 지휘자

heterogeneous 이질적인, 혼성의

thrill 흥분시키다

expansive 활달한, 개방적인

jolly 즐거운, 유쾌한

promenade concert 프롬나드 콘서트(야외 음악회)

intensification 강화, 증대

marvellously 경이적으로

indispensable 없어서는 안 되는, 필수 불가결한

spy out 몰래 탐지하다

respective 각각의

gulf 갈라진 틈, 격차

hautboy 오보에

fiddler 바이올린 연주자

beatific 그지없이 행복한, 기쁨에 넘친

jangle 요란스러운 소리를 내다

vitalising 활력을 주는, 고무시키는

architecture 건축, 건축물

abound 풍부하다

CHAPTER 10

humdrum 지루함, 단조로움

perception 지각, 인식

thoroughly 완전히, 철저히

imbue 스며들게 하다, 불어넣다

heredity 유전, 유전적 형질

comprehensible 이해할 수 있는, 알기 쉬운

bitterness 비통함, 쓰라림

curiousness 묘함

amid …의 한복판에

picturesque 그림 같은, 다채로운

grandiose 웅대한, 장엄한

monotonous 단조로운, 변화 없는

geology 지질학

vapour 수증기

inevitably 피할 수 없이, 필연적으로

liquid 액체

penetrate (사상 등이) 침투하다

durable 오래 가는

cultivate 계발하다, 연마하다

appreciation 인식, 식별, 감지

rents 집세, 임차료

lunch 점심을 먹다

excessive 지나친, 과도한

wigwam 북아메리카 원주민의 오두막

disdainfully 경멸적으로

estate agent 부동산 중개업자

foster 육성하다, 기르다

breathless 숨 가쁜, 흥분되는

enthralling 마음을 사로잡는, 매혹시키는

cellar 지하실

drain 하수구

property 부동산, 토지

favour (이론 등을) 뒷받침하다, 확증하다

breathless 숨 가쁜

disguise 가장하다, 위장하다

enthralling 마음을 사로잡는, 아주 재미있는

pen 우리 안에 가두다, 감금하다

excursion 소풍, 짧은 여행

beat (날개가) 파닥거리다

coordinate 통합하다, 조정하다

superstructure 상부 구조

CHAPTER 11

bent on …에 열중한, 열심인

prose 산문

appreciable 상당한

skiff (한 사람이 노로 젓는) 작은 보트

strain 긴장, 애씀

noonday 정오, 한낮

sackcloth 참회복, 상복

ordeal 시련, 고난

ridicule 비웃음, 조롱

sealed 봉인된

misapprehension 오해, 착오

mediaeval 중세의

torture 고문

pace 한 걸음, 보폭

desirous of …을 바라는

narrative poetry 서사시

infinitely 무한히

verse 운문, 시

antagonistic 적대적인, 상반되는

inconsolably 위로할 수 없을 정도로

vastly 대단히

aught =anything

majestic 위엄 있는, 장엄한, 웅장한

tyro 초심자, 초보자

assault 공략하다, 급습하다

masterpiece 걸작, 명작

lucid 명쾌한, 알기 쉬운

futile 헛된, 효과 없는, 무익한

beforehand 미리, 앞질러

shire 주(州)

fatiguing 피곤하게 하는

CHAPTER 12

terminate 끝내다, 종결시키다

hints 조언, 귀띔

didactic 교훈적인, 설교조의

abrupt (말투가) 퉁명스러운

vegetate 하는 일 없이 지내다

aspirant 큰 뜻을 품은 사람

odious 밉살스러운, 싫은

prig 고상한 체 하는 사람

pert 건방진, 주제넘은

superior 뛰어난, 우세한

pompous 점잔 빼는, 거드름 피우는

attire 옷차림새, 복장

tedious 진저리 나는, 지루한

displeased 화난

fatal 치명적인, 불행을 초래하는

set forth on …에 나서다, 출발하다

roll on 계속 돌다(구르다)

chatter 재잘거리다, 수다를 지껄이다

betray 무심코 드러내다

spectacle 보기에도 딱한 광경, 참상

chariot 전차

fetish 미신의 대상, 물신(物神)

employ 고용

distressing 괴로움을 주는

martyred 순교 당한, 박해 당한

out of the question 불가능한

note 어조, 음성

finality 결정적임, 변경할 수 없음

plaintive 푸념하는

deference 존경, 경의

elasticity 융통성

inexperienced 경험이 없는, 미숙한

rush 분주한 활동

be obsessed by …에 사로잡히다

mend 개선하다, 고치다

run over 초과하다, 흘러 넘치다

cure 해결책, 치료

reconstitute 재구성하다, 재편성하다

oppressive 중압감을 주는, 답답한

modify 변경하다, 수정하다

pallative 완화책

exaggerated 과장된, 비정상적으로 확장된

deliberation 신중함, 찬찬함

portion 부분

quiescence 침묵, 정적

outright 당장, 완전히

impulse 충동, 욕구

lap (경기에서) 한 바퀴

tedium 지겨움, 권태, 지루함

distaste 싫음, 혐오

tiresome 지루한, 따분한, 진저리 나는

inclination 경향, 기질, 기호

street-cries 행상인의 외침 소리